A LITTLE OFF LINE

A Little Off Line

Irreverent essays by Maurice Line,

his friends and colleagues

Illustrations by Mark Bryant

First published in this binding and format by ELM Publications, Seaton House, Kings Ripton, Huntingdon, Cambs PE17 2NJ in September, 1988.

British Library Cataloguing in Publication Data

Line, Maurice B. (Maurice Bernard)
    A little off line.
    1. Librarianship
    I. Title
    020

    ISBN 0-946139-06-7

Printed and bound by St Edmundsbury Press, Bury St Edmunds, Suffolk, England.

CONTENTS

FOREWORD

All agree that professional library literature is far too solemn. I have produced more than my quota of solemnity. Unlike others, however, I have over the years tried to make some amends by writing occasional less solemn pieces, most of them for *New Library World,* under various pseudonyms (to guard my respectability).

This little volume collects together these pieces, with one previously unpublished essay (*Librarianship as it is practised: a failure of intellect, imagination and inititative*) which has a more serious message, albeit not expressed in wholly solemn terms.

Maurice Line

ACKNOWLEDGEMENTS

The sources used for the articles in this book are given below. We would like to acknowledge and thank the owners of the various journals for their permission to reprint; in particular MCB University Press (who publish *New Library World).*

[Frank Windrush] Suck it and see! *New Library World,* 74 (871), January 1973, 6-7.

[Don Lockett] Those wide open spaces. *New Library World,* 74 (874), April 1973, 75-76.

[Austin Rowe] A load of British rubbish. *New Library World,* 75 (883), January 1974, 4-5.

[I Le Mesurier] Advances in library science. *New Library World,* 76 (897), March 1975, 57.

[Inigo Smart] Wider measures. *New Library World,* 76 (898), April 1975, 73-74.

[B. L. Moses] Laws of librarianship. *New Library World,* 82 (972), June 1981, 101.

[B. L. Moses] Fallacies of librarianship. *New Library World,* 83 (979), January 1982, 6; reprinted in *College and Research Libraries News,* 43 (1), January 1982, 13.

[anon.] From Moses to megabytes: a short history of on-line access to information. *UC&R Newsletter,* no. 10 July 1983, 5-6.

[Eunice M. Blair] ISLiP: an imaginative venture. *New Library World,* 87 (1038), October 1986, 186-187.

[Eunice M. Blair] The joy of backlogs. *New Library World,* January 1988.

[Agnew Broome] The search for the ideal. *BLL Review,* 2 (1), January 1974.

BIBLIOPHONICS

BOSTON SYMPHONY ORCHESTRA

William Steinberg	*Music Director*
Michael Tilson Thomas	*Associate Conductor*
Thomas D. Perry Jnr.	*Manager*
Harry J. Kraut	*Associate Manager*

MEMBERS OF THE ORCHESTRA

Earl Hedberg
Joseph Pietropaolo
Robert Barnes
Hironaka Sugie

Chair

Bass Clarinet
Felix Viscuglia

Bassoons
Sherman Walt
Ernst Panenka
Matthew Ruggiero

Contra Bassoon
Richard Plaster

Librarians
Victor Alpert
William Shisler

Horns
James Stagliano
Charles Yancich
Shapiro

SUCK IT AND SEE!

Frank Windrush

A recent programme of a concert given by the Boston Symphony Orchestra listed, as is customary, members of the orchestra. The last column gives Bass Clarinet, Bassoons, Contra-Bassoon, Librarians, Horns, Trumpets, Trombones, etc. From this it is clear that Librarians are instruments of the orchestra, part of the Wind section, and since the Librarian may not be a well known orchestral instrument, some notes on this are perhaps desirable.

The Librarian is indeed a wind instrument, a sort of cross between a woodwind and brass. It exhibits some of the characteristics of both; it is very hard to play in such a way as to produce even a reasonable sound, and requires great skill if it is not to sound appalling. But this problem is less than it might be, because the amount of air coming out of the instrument is usually very much greater than the noise produced.

Librarians are of two general types, male and female. Either form can be blown or sucked, different players preferring to use different modes. The sound they make in each case is quite different; indeed, a skilful player can produce most interesting sounds by alternately blowing and sucking a Librarian.

Within this general division, there are several subdivisions of the instrument. The most commonly seen is the Public Librarian, which can often be seen in large numbers in appropriate surroundings. It is unusual in that the leading instrument is expected not only to be played more skilfully than the rest, but to produce considerably more noise, often of a semi-random nature. From time to time, as with other types of Librarian, instruments are gathered together nationally to form a sort of special orchestra called a conference. At this, instruments are played far more vigorously and noisily than they are when they merely serve as one of many different orchestral instruments. Indeed, one of the reasons why the Librarian is little known as an orchestral

1

instrument is that any sound made on it is inaudible to most people.

Another common type of Librarian is the Special Librarian. This instrument is usually found singly; a great deal of solo music has been written for the instrument, but actual performances are much less common. An older name for this instrument was the Documentalist, and a newer name is the Information Scientist. An orchestra consisting entirely of Information Scientists is known as an Institute. Many people consider that these instruments cannot be satisfactorily combined with any other type of Librarian, and that if this is done discords are liable to result.

Yet another version of the instrument, which is generally considered by its players superior to the others, but which is fitted with fewer technical gadgets for performance, is the University or College Librarian. This is the quietest instrument of all, and, except for leading instruments, it is very rarely audible. Many players on these instruments prefer to practise them in back rooms and never venture into any sort of active performance. A fair amount of music has been written for this instrument, but it is generally considered to be lacking in substance.

The most refined form of the instrument so far developed is called a National Librarian. There are rather fewer of these, and they tend to be concentrated together in groups. It is most often heard in London, though the best virtuoso players, and the most noisy and consistent performers, are found in Yorkshire. There are also Welsh and Scottish versions of this instrument. Apart from the Yorkshire instruments, this particular version is notable for the lack of development it has undergone in the last 200 years.

One particularly interesting thing about Librarians is that male and female instruments can play together, in a mode known as bibliographic coupling. This is considered particularly enjoyable by the players involved, but as it is generally done in private, it is difficult to evaluate performances in this mode.

Some think the instrument is capable of little further development, apart from external decoration, such as has been common with the Special Librarian since the war. This results in a more glamorous looking instrument, but the sound produced is little different from what it was before.

The subject of the Librarian must not be left without some reference to one very special type of instrument, the Cataloguer. This instrument is totally silent, and its continued popularity is hard to understand. It is perhaps characteristic of the Yorkshire National Librarian orchestra that it contains no Cataloguers, though it does contain a rather similar instrument called a Recorder (not to be confused with the other less sonorous instrument of the same name).

Reprinted from:

[Frank Windrush] Suck it and see! *New Library World,* 74 (871), January 1973, 6-7.

THOSE WIDE OPEN SPACES

Don Lockett

The information explosion, the demand for educated manpower at all levels, the pool of untapped ability - these are all clichés in modern Britain, not the less true for being clichés. The formal education system in general fails to communicate fully with the very large proportion of the population commonly, if unhappily, known as 'working class', despite all the modern developments in teaching methods. Books are there for all to read, but all won't read them; the more educational programmes on television are watched mainly by the already educated.

What is needed is constant *exposure* to information: not the forced feeding that often takes place in schools, but an exposure that is unobtrusive and yet inescapable, open to all ages and classes. I believe there is a category of communication media which meets these criteria.

One obvious possibility is the walls of the underground escalator; but these are already well (and presumably lucratively) filled with sources of stimulation rather than information (the information conveyed about the female form and what it wears is surely redundant to all females and most males). A more promising prospect is the dentist's ceiling. Lying back in agony is rarer now than reclining in boredom, mouth numbed and filled with gentle spray. Educational films could be projected on to the ceiling, though the films would have to be very carefully selected beforehand to occupy the same time as the dental treatment; and natural breaks might not always coincide with mouth rinsing. There would be side benefits; the dentist would not have to make cheerful conversation, and the patient would not have to leave his questions unanswered or his assertions unchallenged. Another possibility is the doctor's waiting room; films would not be so suitable for this as wall posters, which would have to be such that sudden interruption did not matter greatly.

However, there is one unexploited information medium of far

greater potential than dentists' ceilings or doctors' walls - the public lavatory wall. This potential is of course already used to some extent; lavatory walls all over the country are covered with writings which are read by countless people. However, these writings convey an exceedingly limited range of information; moreover, within these limits some of the information is inaccurate, and much is autobiographical. Indeed lavatory walls are used not so much as media of information as means of self-expression by the writers.

Before we leave the inadequacies of the present uses of lavatory walls, we should note that the writings they contain form a vast mine of material for the scholar. Those who write on lavatory walls are probably people who hardly ever write anything else; think of the sociological, aesthetic, psychological and linguistic analysis to which this material could be subjected! The limitation of subject matter has some positive advantages in that regional comparisons could more easily be made; for example, spelling variants of the same words could be studied. The misguided officials who aim to make the walls of a texture and colour that cannot be used for writing are in fact trying to deprive the world of important archives, for no good reason. There are much worse media for self-expression than lavatory walls. In making an alternative proposal for their use, I am not advocating the total abolition of their present purpose; but in any case the government, or some charitable foundation, should certainly initiate and finance a project to photograph lavatory walls all over the country, with the aim of forming a National Inventory and Photographic Record of Lavatory Walls (NIPROLAV). One or two universities could perhaps turn their Departments of Extra-Mural Studies (threatened by the Open University) into Departments of Mural Studies.

The fact that the present use of lavatory walls is not so unfortunate as many assume does not mean that they could not be put to a better use. The advantages they possess as media for educational material are striking. First, they are large, and can therefore take information not only in great quantities but in various forms - drawings, maps, and graphs as well as print. Secondly, in the cubicles (which should be renamed carrels in conformity with library usage) one can remain for a fair time without disturbance or distraction - one of the few places outside one's home where complete privacy is possible. Thirdly, the mind is often in a wonderfully receptive mood in such places. I do not wish here to speculate on the reasons for this, only to suggest that it is unlikely to be due solely to the privacy and seclusion of the surroundings; maybe output creates room for input. At any rate, there is no question that generations have found them uniquely suited to contemplation.

If these walls are covered with *educational* material, it would be next to impossible for some of it not to be conveyed to receptive (and even unreceptive) minds. It has been shown that television has often, despite itself, enlarged people's knowledge and awareness, and often induced them to go to libraries or buy books to follow up something that has caught their interest. This would probably happen to an even greater degree with lavatory walls. Obviously much research is needed to establish the best form, content, educational level and layout of lavatory walls for this purpose, but this research would be of more easily demonstrable value than much educational research currently carried out.

One set of three walls (the rear wall of the carrel would be of little use, except perhaps for containing the answers to questions), can contain so much information that, initially at least, some twenty basic patterns would be sufficient for the whole country. Within one lavatory (re-named **LIBROLAV**) each carrel could be different, so that regular learners could have plenty of variety. Eventually some change of wall would be necessary, if only to keep up with advancing knowledge. This presents something of a technical challenge. Perhaps the 'learning walls' could be clipped to structural walls; or the complete units might be interchangeable.

A programmed learning element could readily be built into the situation. One could thus have a Programmed Learning Lavatory. Answers could be required to appropriate questions, and the delivery of toilet paper would depend on pushing the correct button for the answer. Manufacturers could surely be persuaded to produce a **TUTOLAV**. Indeed, getting out of the carrel at all

7

might be made dependent on correct answers; so long as there were not too many choices allowed for multiple-choice questions, departure would not be delayed long enough to cause hardship to the learner (or waiting learners). If, at a later stage in their learning, pupils wished to test their knowledge, they could use the paper provided and put it in a special receptacle for transmission to, and comment by, a tutor. (Following current practice, appointments with tutors would be made by leaving notes on the walls - another use perhaps for the rear wall.) The whole project - Self-Help Information Transfer Experiment - could be linked to the Open University.

Some improvements in lavatory conditions would be necessary. The lighting is usually very poor, and the physical comfort could definitely be improved; in particular, some more comfortable leaning surface than a narrow pipe is required. Carrels must not however be made too comfortable, otherwise occupants may fall asleep, or keep other would-be learners waiting an unduly long time. More lavatories, and more commodious lavatories, would be needed to cater for the increased average length of stay and, it must be hoped, for the increase in numbers of people wishing to educate themselves in this way. The cost of this would be more than offset by the tremendous educational benefits.

There is of course no reason why the project should be confined to *public* lavatories. Factories could have special walls made to help workers increase their background knowledge or improve their technical efficiency. School lavatories, shop lavatories, directors' lavatories, solicitors' lavatories...the possibilities are endless.

Looking to the future when the librolav with its educational lavatory walls is fully established, one can imagine a new generation of wandering poor scholars who, deprived of reasonable educational opportunity as children, travel from town to town armed with their pennies in search of new lavatory walls to study. In some of them a spark of inspiration would be kindled which would result in new art and literature being given to the world. In their wake would go critics and scholars, studying their walls and possibly even collecting them. New Fraternities would come into

8

being, creating and spreading a new popular culture. Indeed, the Open University might be rivalled by a Privy University.

The prospects are exciting. All that is needed to start off the project is moral support from an enlightened local authority and financial support from a charitable foundation.

Reprinted from:

[Don Lockett] Those wide open spaces. *New Library World,* 74 (874), April 1973, 75-76.

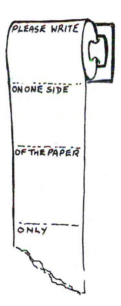

" JUST AS MOSES RECEIVED THE TABLETS
FROM GOD, SO LIBRARIANS RECEIVED A
SET OF CATALOGUING RULES... "

THE SEARCH FOR THE IDEAL

Agnew Broome

The search for the ideal is a continuing element in human history. Without ideals, few advances would be made. However, unwillingness to accept anything but the ideal constitutes in its extreme form a neurosis, perhaps totally incapacitating the person who suffers from it. Librarianship has been, and is, afflicted with a version of this disease. The central feature is the inability to reduce standards, however arbitrary the standards and whatever the current circumstances. The library system is designed around these standards, which are inviolable, the fixed elements in an otherwise adaptable system. How this operates can best be shown by examples.

The best example is the catalogue. Just as Moses received the tablets from God, so librarians received a set of cataloguing rules from a scarcely less august body, namely a committee specially constructed to frame them. The general principle underlying the rules is that all possible contingencies should be provided for in all entries for all books. In fact, this ideal was not attained, presumably because some portions of common sense entered the heads of a least some of those framing the rules, or, more probably perhaps, because no-one had happened to think of additional elements that might be included, such as the colour of a book etc. The rules were framed without any attempt to assess usability of catalogue entries, to identify by actual study of users the elements that were needed at all, or those that could perhaps be dispensed with because they satisfied only a very small percentage of demands (which could in any case be satisfied in other ways), or to calculate the cost of including different elements. The background to the rules was one therefore of folk wisdom ('the accumulated experience of librarians') and tradition ('well established practices').

In addition to the attempt to make the information in catalogue entries 'complete', many if not most libraries attempt to make all details fully accurate. A spelling mistake, even one that is quite obviously a mistake for an identifiable word, an incorrect pagination, a wrong abbreviation for 'frontispiece', things such as this are cardinal sins, worse even than splitting infinitives. Each entry made by a cataloguer has therefore to be checked by someone else for accuracy, preferably by two other people. When catalogue records are received from elsewhere, eg BNB cards, it is desirable to check these also, as it is possible with detailed checking to find errors on 1% of cards.

Apart from the cost of perfection of this kind, it can usually be demonstrated to be ineffective even on its own terms, as two cataloguers, following precisely the same set of rules, will produce catalogue entries differing in trivial, sometimes even important, ways for the same book. Indeed, the same cataloguer cataloguing the same book on different days would probably not achieve even 90% consistency. Nevertheless, so long as the cataloguer satisfies his own perfectionism, it does not matter much whether he satisfies anyone else, even another cataloguer - certainly not the user, who may for all we know be just as well served by very simple catalogue entries containing multiple minor errors. Indeed, he might well be *better* served, because a simple catalogue might be easier to use.

The quest for perfection can, and often does, result in very large backlogs of cataloguing. It is often not uncommon to see backlogs of anything from 6 months to 2 years in libraries, particularly academic libraries. Never mind whether the readers are waiting for the books, or whether the funds will ever be available, for cataloguing them properly; *standards must not be reduced.* In fact, in the search for one ideal another ideal has been completely forgotten: service to the user. If this were taken as the ideal, and if the financial and practical constraints were accepted as real constraints (as indeed they are), libraries might begin to think how they could serve the user most effectively. At present, the situation is parallel to that of the man who is extremely hungry, but who would rather starve to death because he cannot find the ideal meal to eat in perfectly hygienic conditions.

Similar considerations apply to classification. Attempts continue to find the perfect classification scheme, in apparent unawareness that the structure of knowledge changes, and that even if a perfect classification scheme were found, it would not be perfect for long. Meanwhile, librarians have several schemes from which to choose. So far as is known, there is virtually nothing to choose between these as a way of arranging books on shelves. However, one librarian who takes charge of a library arranged by Dewey decides that Library of Congress is superior, or vice versa, and proceeds to re-classify the whole stock. This operation has three consistent features: it absorbs a very large amount of staff effort, it takes an immensely long time, and it makes complete chaos of the library while it is being done. There is always the chance (perhaps even probability) that the operation will not be finished by the time the librarian retires or moves elsewhere, and that his successor may then decide to revert to the original scheme or adopt a third scheme, thereby compounding chaos.

Ready-made Dewey numbers are available for British books through BNB. However, most libraries find it necessary to check these, both for accuracy and for local applicability. With sufficient thought, it is possible to improve or modify any classification number. It is certainly true that no national classification can meet all local needs perfectly, but it is equally true that the 'bad' cases will constitute only a tiny minority, and that the cost of checking all classification numbers almost certainly outweighs any benefit gained from altering a few.

One further factor is the desire to make the same thing serve more than one purpose, even when the purposes are totally different and sometimes inconsistent. This applies to cataloguing: most librarians will admit that the main function of their catalogue is as a finding list, but they will argue 'but if we enrich it in certain ways it can serve as a bibliography'. Similarly, a shelf classification can provide a sort of subject access; if sufficiently refined, as in UDC, it can operate as a moderately sophisticated retrieval tool. However, the result is usually that the classification finally adopted is neither adequate for retrieval nor fully usable as a method of shelf arrangement, because the numbers and symbols are too long, insufficiently memorable, etc.

The same perfectionism pervades many acquisition systems, which have had built into them many checks to ensure, for example, that it is possible 10 years after a book has been acquired to find out what its original price is if it is lost, to ensure that no duplicates ever slip through, to ensure that no supplier ever gets away with a single mistake, etc. Even with the most sloppy acquisition system, the number of duplicates that will enter the system, as a percentage of all acquisitions, will be trivial, and their cost very small, usually far smaller than the cost of constant checking, not to mention the delays that this may produce.

Issue systems sometimes suffer from the same 100% syndrome. They are able to provide very large amounts of information, most of which are hardly ever used. In the worst cases, the reader has to provide all these details himself. When challenged, the circulation librarian can almost always quote a case that happened several months ago when a particular element of information proved to be invaluable to answer an important question. A temptation, when this happens, is to give examples of additional elements of information that might also have answered important questions, but this is a dangerous thing to do, since the circulation librarian may not previously have thought of this and may proceed to add it to the system for the future.

Unbound periodicals are messy things, and it is held essential to bind them as soon as possible. Otherwise, covers come off, parts get lost, etc. Unfortunately, the binding operation nearly always takes place at the time of maximum usage, when the articles in them appear in the indexing and abstracting tools, and are heavily referred to by articles in other journals. The user's convenience is once again being sacrificed to the fear of an incomplete set and the desire to have neatly bound volumes standing on the shelves. It goes without saying that the style of binding and lettering used within a set must not vary in the least degree: a change of colour, or a ¼ in. difference in height of lettering, is unacceptable.

Stocktaking is another operation which is accepted as necessary in most libraries. If possible, the entire stock is checked against the catalogues. As a result, some books are found to be missing that were already known to be missing. In addition, some books are found to be missing that were not known to be missing, because no-one has subsequently wanted them. Moreover, errors in the catalogue are discovered, in particular entries are found for books that no longer exist, or no entries are found for books that do exist. One characteristic of the perfectionist is that in order to live with his own perfectionism, and knowing that he cannot attain it himself, he must find others who are also imperfect, preferably more imperfect than himself. Few things therefore so rejoice the librarian as when in stocktaking he comes across someone else's mistake, be it large or small.

One trouble with the 100% syndrome is that it limits the options available (usually to one). Retrospective conversion of catalogues to machine-readable form is an example. If the only worthwhile aim is held to be the total conversion of all entries with full, and preferably revised, entries, the cost may and probably will rule it out. But there are many other options: to 'freeze' the catalogue, to convert short records only and use the existing catalogue as a backstop, or printed bibliographies as a backstop, to use short records available from elsewhere, and so on.

Many more examples could be quoted of library operations that aim at 100%, and inconvenience readers to a greater or lesser degree. However, one major example of the 100% syndrome cannot be omitted - the quest for self-sufficiency in stock. Alas, facts have caught up with even the most perfectionist librarian, and no librarian now claims that his stock is self-sufficient; reluctantly, he borrows from elsewhere, lamenting the extent of this borrowing in his annual report, and using it as an argument for increased funds. Nevertheless, attitudes die hard, and there is a considerable hangover from the self-sufficiency era. This persists in the 'more voluminous that thou' complex - the use, as a standard measure of comparison between libraries, of the number of volumes a library holds, as if bulk is somehow a measure of quality. With libraries, as with women, sheer bulk should be totally irrelevant as a measure of quality: the real measure by which libraries should be judged is the percentage of demands they can satisfy (I would not care to speculate whether this also applies to women). Nevertheless, libraries will still accept vast donations of material of which only a fraction will ever be used, and record it gratefully in their annual reports. Reports of this kind should add that the acquisition of this material will occupy a large amount of space in the library, thus hastening the need for a new building or increasing pressure on the existing one, and will also absorb a good deal of effort on the part of the cataloguers, thus possibly increasing the backlog of current cataloguing.

As stated above, the true measure of library service, by which all elements of the service must eventually be judged, is the service it offers its clientele. Whether they like it or not, libraries have to operate within certain constraints, of buildings, staffing, funds, etc. The real aim of a library should be to maximise the service to users within these constraints; or, better still, to draw cost-effectiveness curves for all library operations, showing clearly where the cut-off point occurs, that is where an increase in effectiveness becomes much smaller than the necessary increase in costs. Budgeting can then be put on a firm basis. This would *not,* in most libraries at any rate, result in reduced financial resources: most libraries that seriously tried to measure their effectiveness would find (as one or two libraries have already found) that they fell well short of it, and that, when they had cut off the waste that every system has, they still needed additional resources to give a proper cost-effective service. They would in fact be in a far better position to claim for funds than they have been in the past.

To summarise, the quest for the ideal in libraries has led to perfectionist paralysis - an inability to accept facts as they are, and hope that somehow facts will change to meet the desired situation. More seriously, *the wrong ideal has been pursued:* the perfection of the system in itself, rather than the service given to the users.

Note: Some librarians may suffer from a 'more radical than thou' complex, which may have its own devastating consequences.

Reprinted from:

[Agnew Broome] The search for the ideal. *BLL Review,* 2 (1), January 1974.

A LOAD OF BRITISH RUBBISH

Austin Rowe

Now that the British Library is in being, it is up to the library community to consider whether it is playing its full roles in the library life of the country. After all, the powers vested in it by the British Library Act are considerable. It is up to every librarian to work out and put forward his own ideas; I wish here to make two suggestions.

The first is merely an extension of a proposal that has already been made. The national provision of printed ephemera in the social sciences was the subject of a report by John Pemberton a year or two ago. However, this goes no further than advocating the collection on a much more comprehensive scale than hitherto of printed documents that are intended to serve only a temporary purpose. The future historian will not want to depend only on printed or even manuscript documents; to find out how we lived from day to day (and from night to night) he will want evidence of a more earthy kind.

The prehistorian's best evidence for reconstructing the life of early peoples is often the middens that have been preserved by some chance or another. What would not a prehistorian give for a whole systematic collection of individual middens, in mint condition?

We owe it to posterity to preserve the evidence of our daily life. True, municipal rubbish tips are likely to be preserved, owing to our habit of covering them over with soil when they are mature; but before that the rubbish of numerous people, shops, hotels etc, has been mixed together and incinerated, and what is left will not help much in the reconstruction of the lives of individuals, with their individual variety. For this, what is needed is a random sample of dustbins. From a content analysis of a dustbin, it is not too difficult, with a little imagination, to piece together the life of an individual or a family over a week (if you don't believe this, have a look at your own dustbin and think what a private detective could make of it).

Sampling would have to be done systematically. The sample would be stratified by region and social class, and collection would be made (without special warning) at different times of year. Ideally, the information would include the age and occupation of the dustbin fillers. All dustbins would be labelled, indexed and put immediately into deep freeze. Imagine the joy of the future historian when he finds the dustbin of a Buckinghamshire stockbroker aged 56 (Spring 1973), of a Notting Hill housewife aged 35 (Autumn 1974), or of a Scottish public librarian aged 50 (Summer 1965); when he has the dustbins brought out of deep freeze and is able to explore their contents with his own hands.

The collection of dustbins would be a fairly straightforward matter; a little extra pay to dustmen should ensure this is done adequately. The main problem is likely to be storage. Dustbins in large numbers take up a lot of space; this could probably be found in a worked out mine or quarry, but deep freezing a very large area would undoubtedly be costly. This is a matter of priorities. Do we care enough about our future to be willing to hand it down in a tangible form to posterity? Is it less worthwhile to preserve dustbins than some buildings which are already decaying and which cost a great deal to conserve? Do we care so little about our rubbish that we are not willing to establish the world's first National Refuse Collection?

My second suggestion is equally practicable, but would serve the needs of the near rather than the distant future. The personality of librarians has been studied more than once, most notably in the United States and Australia, and we seem to be a funny lot. This is the experience too of many chief librarians, whether in recruiting staff or in trying to introduce change with existing staff. Librarians appear to be in general nice, stable, helpful people but lacking in drive, rather introverted, and not very good at harnessing intelligence to getting things done; with the result that what progress there has been has been forced upon us by our masters or has come about as the result of ideas from outside the profession. The professional image is not good either, and it cannot be changed without some change in the people employed, even if it is not entirely true that no female librarian has ever discovered Smirnoff without leaving the profession for one that

20

appears to be still older, or, as is implied, that all women still employed in libraries are Good Girls.

Much thought has been given to ways in which we can improve the quality of librarians, but one idea has not, so far as I know, so far been put forward.

Why do we not *breed our own librarians?* This would require the identification of existing librarians agreed to be of high calibre, and their mating with women selected as having the qualities of which librarianship is short. It would not of course be guaranteed that all their produce would go into librarianship, whatever special rewards were offered them, nor indeed that all would reproduce the qualities of their parents, because of the phenomenon of regression to the mean (most clearly seen in intelligence testing; the average IQ of the offspring of a couple tends to be halfway between the average of the IQs of the parents and 100, the mean of all IQs in the population). Nevertheless, there is a good chance that, say, a quarter of the children will in due course contribute to librarianship much of what it now appears to lack.

Careful planning would be necessary to ensure the success of this operation - let us call it the National Library Stud. The best method of picking the stallions would perhaps be by consensus of chief libarians in all kinds of library (self-marking excluded). Payment would be inappropriate; outstanding performance could be rewarded by a special medal (suggestions for a suitable name for the medal invited), or, perhaps more appropriately, by an extra mare. Initial selection of mares would be by personality tests (LA qualifications an additional advantage, as they say), further selection by willingness and desirability. Since Nurture is important as well as Nature, the children would have to be brought up in suitable conditions, perhaps in one of the divisions of the British Library.

On the question of staffing, it is surprising that there has been almost no application of systems design to the appointment and allocation of individuals to particular jobs. Readers may care to know of a recent study carried out for a library which has asked to remain nameless. The aim was to state, and fulfil, the design

21

requirements of a female library assistant, with the main duties related to the lending library. To serve at the issue desk, she should be able to handle books on issue and return while sitting. She should therefore have a long body and long arms, to reach over the counter. For reshelving books, she must reach all the shelves, from those at 7ft. 6in. to those near the floor. Her long body and arms would be able to cope with the top shelves, but if she also had long legs she would have to do an exceptional amount of stooping to reach the bottom shelves. A further requirement was therefore seen to be for short legs.

These were then the minimum specifications as laid down by the special team entrusted with the study. There were however further desiderata. For maximum leaning across the counter, a flat chest would be preferable; this would also enable her to carry a pile of books without the upper part of the pile being thrust forward. The long arms and body would of course maximise book holding capacity, but this would be useless without strong body, arm and leg muscles. For maximum stability, her legs should be thick as well as strong, otherwise the point of balance of her body would be well above her hips. A strong and prominent chin was also desirable, to keep the pile of books in place.

Finally, readers must be both greeted pleasantly when they return books, and deterred from abuse of the library. Conventional prettiness is in any case out of the question, as it encourages use of the library for other purposes than reading, and causes waste of time through constant chatting-up; in severe cases, staff leave to get married, whether for preference or necessity. The solution seemed to lie in features which are pleasant but which can be turned to a severe look if required.

The team is well satisfied with its work; indeed, it believes it may have broken new ground, since the study, so far from being an ordinary ergonomic exercise, which aims to design tasks, desks, chairs etc, to fit people, attempted instead to design people for the work and fittings. The library too is very pleased with the study. It has however not yet succeeded in finding staff to fit the stated requirements; if any female reader happens to fit them, they are asked to get in touch with the Editor of *New Library World.*

Reprinted from:

[Austin Rowe]   A load of British rubbish. *New Library World,* 75 (883), January 1974,
4-5.

ADVANCES IN LIBRARY SCIENCE

I le Mesurier

BIBLIOMETRICS has now, for better or worse, become an accepted term for an accepted activity - the collection and analysis of statistical data on literature. To the librarian's principle, 'If you don't understand it, classify it, then you'll feel safer', has been added the information scientist's 'If you don't understand it, measure it'.

Collecting masses of figures, carrying out sophisticated analyses and computations, constructing complex tables and drawing graphs are peculiarly soothing activities, like knitting. (Indeed, statistics can be very like a kind of intellectual knitting.) There is, of course, a danger that measurement becomes a substitute for rather than an aid to comprehension, that no decisions are made until measurement has been undertaken, and that therefore everything is measured.

In a recent Aslib paper, Dr Urquhart gave as a hypothetical example of silly measurement the calculation of what proportion of librarians had red hair. This suggested to me a new branch of library and information science - *Bibliothecariometrics,* or the *Measurement of librarians.* So far from being useless, I can see great value in this new study.

A first step would be to draw up a list of all characteristics of librarians amenable to statistical calculation and analysis. Among attributes would be colours of hair, eye and skin; pitch of voice; and, of course, sex. Variables would include vital physical statistics as well as age. I am not here considering education and other background characteristics, since some attention has been given to these already; I am concerned only with the librarian as he/she is here and now.

The geographical distribution of, say, green-eyed red-haired women librarians of medium height would be fascinating information. If it proved non-random, the library press could be filled with articles speculating why. It might come down to the fact that one or two librarians in a certain area happened to have a special taste for these characteristics, and that they had made a sort of special collection of them. Similar explanations might account for a preponderance of long legs and large breasts in certain localities. (Inevitably one is led on to *Bibliothecariopsychometry,* but that must be the subject of another paper.)

Lest the foregoing should be considered mere male chauvinist piggery, I can provide evidence that these interests are not necessarily confined to male librarians: I once worked under a female librarian who suggested that I try to persuade a certain slender female member of the library staff to join a choral society in the hope that it might develop her bust. In any case, female bosses are presumably just as interested in male librarians - it's just that I know less about the details of their interest.

Bibliothecariometric studies are of far more interest if one type of library is compared with another, one country with another, and, perhaps of particular interest, one period of time with another. Are librarians' legs getting longer, eyes getting greener? Of even more interest and importance would it be to compare librarians with other professions. Are we getting our fair shares of Apollos and Aphrodites, or for that matter Pans and Gorgons?

Much library and information research can be rather boring, and partly for this reason it is not easy to attract people into it. Bibliothecariometric research would be a different matter altogether. Studying hair colours might become tedious after a time, but gazing into eyes should be rewarding. However, it is the physical measurement that would really appeal to researchers. I do not need to draw attention to the interest, and occasional outstanding pleasure, of measuring legs and chests.

There would be a valuable spin-off from this research. Librarians have been reputed to be rather introverted, perhaps a little neurotic. Encounter groups, with their physical contact, have had beneficial effects in some such cases. Physical measurement would not be precisely similar to encounter group contact, but the effects and benefits might be comparable. Indeed, data collection need not be confined to a few researchers, but could be widely shared out, thus extending the data while spreading the pleasure. Mutual Measurement Meetings might become a standard part of library conferences. (I am not suggesting that library conferences are entirely devoid of physical contact now, but it can hardly claim to be directed to the advancement of knowledge.)

Let Bibliothecariometrics commence: a new branch of knowledge, harmless, interesting and enjoyable. Of how much current library research can this be said?

Reprinted from:

[I Le Mesurier] Advances in library science. *New Library World*, 76 (897), March 1975, 57.

WIDER MEASURES

Inigo Smart

Bibliothecariometrics need and should not be confined to physical characteristics, as Mr le Mesurier seems to imply in his pioneering article last month. The Bradford distribution as applied to library uses and citations is now well known. A relatively small percentage of books or references (maybe 20%) account for a high proportion (maybe 80%) of use. The implications of this are that the long 'tail' of the distribution can be disposed of, or not acquired, by libraries: if they acquire, or retain, the critical 20%, they are optimizing the use of their resources.

The same distribution can be observed at any committee meeting. 10% or 20% of the members contribute 80% of the discussion. Since attendance at committee meetings is expensive, the long 'tail' of silent or near silent members can be dispensed with; this would save very large sums of money, and probably make it unnecessary to have any increase in the Library Association's subscriptions for at least 10 years, during which a handsome surplus could be built up. The identification of the 'core' would be a simple process.

There is however another factor to be taken into account; the noise-to-signal ratio. It is true that articles and books differ widely in their noise-to-signal ratio, but there is usually some vetting procedure before they get published, and in any case uses or citations are likely to be concentrated on the best signals rather than the loudest noises. With committee members it is not so simple. It is well known that the number of words is often in inverse proportion to the meaning communicated - if indeed any meaning is communicated at all. Nor is the number of contributions made a good measure of value. Developing a noise-to-signal measure for committee discussions should be a high priority for bibliothecariometric research, but the weeding of committees need not await the results of this research, for it can be safely said that those who say nothing at all contribute nothing at all (usually not even ornamental value), and these at least could be removed. If the threat of removal provoked them into opening their mouths, who knows what pearls might emerge?

It may be objected that the removal of non-productive members would mean that some categories of library, or areas of the country, or whatever, were unrepresented. This need not be so. The Library Association could keep a supply of inflatable plastic committee members (IPCMs), who could be labelled with the category of library or areas they represented, and who could form an imposing presence at meetings. The danger of punctures could add to their interest and value; if puncture proneness could be built into them, all eyes would turn from time to time to the inflated members to watch for shrinkage. Models could be designed to emit low moans, high squeaks, gasps or a whole variety of other noises as they expired. These emissions could be minuted, and might be found to come at very appropriate points in the discussion. (Who has not experienced a sneeze, a cough, or a stomach rumble as the most valuable contribution to a meeting?) The highlight of a committee meeting will of course be an instant explosion of an over-inflated member. (In case anyone wonders, I am assured by the Library Association that it is not using IPCMs already).

IPCMs would be of particular value at international conferences, where they could be transported and maintained very cheaply, and inflated for meetings where a Presence was necessary. IFLA would be transformed by such a measure, and its problems of reorganization solved at a stroke (or rather, at a blow). I should be astonished if a cost benefit analysis did not work out overwhelmingly in favour of this proposal. I hereby challenge the Library Association to commission one.

Reprinted from:

[Inigo Smart] Wider measures. *New Library World,* 76 (898), April 1975, 73-74

LAWS OF LIBRARIANSHIP

B L Moses

The efficiency of a library is in inverse relation to the proportion of expenditure accounted for by staff and the proportion of staff accounted for by cataloguers.

The number of interpretations of any catalogue rule is the square root of the number of times it is applied.

Any cataloguing rule takes fifteen people ten years to produce. It needs revision ten years after publication, unless it is easy to understand and apply, in which case it is revised five years after publication. Each revision takes fifteen people ten years to make and is out of date ten years after publication...

75% of the use of any catalogue is by cataloguers for the purpose of adding to it.

Catalogues expand beyond the cabinets available.

The esteem in which a classification scheme is held bears an inverse relation to the number of libraries using it.

The reputation of a librarian bears a direct relation to the number of his publications.

The ability of a librarian bears no relation to the number of his publications.

The extent of acceptance of a library theory or practice bears no relation to its validity.

The average height of chief university librarians shall be greater than the average height of other university library staff, except in the case of females, when it shall be lesser.

The average weight of chief public librarians shall be greater than the average weight of other public library staff, except in the case of females, when it shall be lesser.

The weight of a chief librarian's secretary shall be more than twice the square root of his weight, except in the case of female chief librarians, when the converse shall apply.

Reprinted from:

[B. L. Moses] Laws of librarianship. *New Library World,* 82 (972), June 1981, 101.

FALLACIES OF LIBRARIANSHIP

B L Moses

1.   Users can find their own way around a library.

2.   Users are completely helpless at all stages of library use.

3.   Gift books are free.

4.   Cooperation between libraries, of whatever kind, saves money.

5.   Holdings are more important than service.

6.   The case for well-funded libraries is self-apparent.

7.   A library that receives no complaints is a good library.

8.   Library education is a useful preparation for library practice.

9.   A research library should give the unknown needs of the future priority over the known needs of the present.

10.   The catalogue is the key to the library.

11.   Interlibrary borrowing is expensive.

12.   Interlibrary borrowing is a cheap substitute for acquisition.

13.   Interlibrary borrowing is no substitute for acquisition.

14.   The distance between a lending and a borrowing library affects the speed of supply.

15.   It is possible to devise a classification scheme that

organizes knowledge in a coherent, useful, and intelligible way that is and will remain acceptable.

16. Existing classification schemes can be improved by local modification.

17. No system devised for one library can be adopted by any other library.

18. A love of books is a useful prerequisite for a librarian.

19. All that is needed to improve a library service is more money and more staff.

20. A library building that wins a prize for architecture is functional.

Reprinted from:

[B. L. Moses] Fallacies of Librarianship. *New Library World,* 83 (979), January 1982, 6; reprinted in *College and Research Libraries News,* 43 (1), January 1982, 13.

FROM MOSES TO MEGABYTES: A SHORT HISTORY OF ONLINE ACCESS TO INFORMATION

[Anon]

Moses was having trouble with his followers' morals. They kept on coveting their neighbours' wives and asses (usually in that order), working on the seventh day, and making graven images, not to mention stealing, committing adultery and killing. He issued guidelines from time to time and introduced sanctions, but they all gave the impression of improvisation. He needed something more authoritative.

So he thought he would go and log on to the ultimate source of wisdom, the Great Online Database (GOD), sometimes also called the Grand Old Datalink. The only terminal within reasonable reach was up a mountain, where it was safer from vandalism and unofficial use. (There was another terminal, made by Bush, which caught fire and came to be remembered as the Burning Bush, but the less said about that the better). Moses was a bit rusty with the procedures, but the system was user-friendly and interactive, and Moses was soon able to say what he needed - a fairly short set of rules. One by one they were displayed on the terminal.

'Oh GOD', keyed in Moses, 'I'll never remember all that, and in any case the people will need some proof. Can I have a printout?'

'Regret only form of material available at your terminal as a physical printout medium', replied GOD, 'is stone'.

'That will have to do' keyed in Moses.

So, with the old fashioned chisel printers around in those days, the stones were slowly engraved with the Ten Commandments, and Moses struggled slowly down the mountain with them. The people were convinced, and felt more guilty therafter when they coveted, worked on the seventh day, etc. etc.

The stone printout had the excellent feature of permanence but was very heavy to carry around, and as Moses had to keep moving from one place to another, he began to look around for a lighter substitute. His mind went back to his earliest infancy. The bulrushes wouldn't do, but what about the papyrus nearby? That proved to be just the thing, although the ink tended to run when they crossed the river or whenever the heavens opened. So they built a shrine .... (this was the first library, though it wasn't called that).

Centuries passed. The terminal on Mount Sinai became obsolete, and in their wanderings and battles the Hebrews forsook GOD - indeed, they lost all knowledge of the system. Various writing materials were tried, but they tended to be fragile like papyrus or expensive like velum. So the Chinese invented paper. Scrolls proved a nuisance, and separate sheets kept getting out of order, so someone found a way of sewing and sticking them together and called it a CODEX (Collection Of Documents EXtremely handy). Although there wasn't exactly a labour stortage in China (or anywhere else) to produce multiple copies the Chinese also invented printing and the Europeans went and did the same. Books proliferated. These were for the intellectuals, and to keep a more and more literate public fed with information (and gossip) newspapers were started. Authors grew in number and self-importance, and although they liked to be read they were more concerned just to see their works printed.

The world's forests began to disappear faster than new trees could be planted. Library shelves overflowed. Bibliographies were created to provide more control over the vast and increasing quantities of printed material, and these grew even faster in number and size than the printed material they tried to control. Librarians grew in number and self-importance. Microfilm was invented but served as an additional rather than alternative medium, ideal for totally unreadable material.

Users were in despair. They couldn't keep track of *what* was being produced that they ought to read, let alone find time to read it, and when they wanted something badly they couldn't always get it quickly enough, especially as their libraries failed more and more dismally to keep pace with world output. Abstracts were invented, but these whetted users' appetites still more without really satisfying them, like advertisements for unavailable goods.

Meanwhile computers were invented. They were used to produce bibliographies more quickly and with more up to date indexes. These consumed an ever-increasing proportion of library budgets, so that they could afford to buy even less of the literature covered by the bibliographies. So the bibliographies were made available online, which cost so much that the money available to buy literature was still further reduced. Librarians were in despair.

Publishers too were in despair, and started to make their products available online in the hope of building up a second market alongside the failing one for printed literature. Access cost so much that ...

Alternative media were now competing for the market - various forms of sound and vision, and mixtures of sound and vision. The world was overflowing with information.

Meanwhile, up in the heavens, satellites had begun to reappear (GOD was of course accessed via a satellite all those thousands of years ago). Information could be transmitted from almost anywhere instantly (although so far as I know Mount Sinai still hasn't replaced its long-lost terminal). Users were now completely confused with all the quantity, richness and variety of information available, and sought help. What we need, they cried, is a prophet who will tell us what to access and will access it for us.

The wheel had come full circle.

Reprinted from:

[anon.] From Moses to megabytes: a short history of on-line access to information. *UC&R Newsletter,* no. 10 July 1983, 5-6.

"BIBLIOGRAPHERS PLAYING WITH THEIR BIBLIOGRAPHIC TOOLS WHILE USERS REMAIN UNSATISFIED"

LIBRARIANSHIP AS IT IS PRACTISED - A FAILURE OF INTELLECT, IMAGINATION AND INITIATIVE

Maurice B Line

It is becoming generally accepted that the future of developed countries lies largely in their becoming information societies, even information economies, deriving most of their wealth not from manufacturing but from the provision and transmission of information, in its widest sense - from primary education to advertising. At the same time, in nearly all these same countries the resources devoted to libraries, in both public and private sectors, are being cut back, often savagely. Either libraries are doing the wrong things or they have not convinced their lords and masters that they are doing the right things. Something is badly wrong. This paper tries to explore what it is. When making notes for it I soon realized that I could write a book on the subject (and may do so one day); all I can do here is to present the outline of my case, inevitably selective and over-simplified, but I hope not superficial: I warn you that my title is intended to be serious. You will also be glad to know that my text is written on acid-free paper.

There are many problems facing librarianship. The challenge of reduced resources is one of them. Rapidly changing technology is another. Deeper than either are changes in society, both within countries and globally. Some of these problems are closer than others; some are already upon us. I would argue that in most cases librarians have *failed to anticipate* the problems, they have *failed to see problems in context,* they have *failed to identify* the problems correctly and precisely, and when they have been confronted with problems they cannot avoid they have *failed to react intelligently.*

My first example is an easy one, because it is already partly past history. It has been obvious for the last 20 years that academic libraries could not keep being provided with accommodation to keep pace with their intake. When a few of us tried to point this out in Britain and to urge that a great deal of factual evidence was needed on growth rates, costs, the value of browsing, improved means of access to remote stored material, and alternative national solutions to the coming space crisis, we were greeted with attitudes of 'we don't believe it', 'the UGC will provide', 'we'll wait till it happens', 'I'm retiring in 10 years anyway', and 'technology will find a solution'. When the UGC set up the Atkinson Committee, university libraries still did nothing, though when the committee reported they were only too ready to complain that it did not have enough hard evidence - which is perfectly true, because some of the important evidence needed to be collected over several years. Immediately rebuttals began to appear, containing facts and figures of highly dubious quality and not addressing the real problem, which was simply that buildings could not keep pace with growth. The UGC set up a Steering Committee on Library Research, which, after several years of discussion and the collection of more and more information, came to no conclusions that contradicted the Atkinson Report. Libraries are now improvising, mostly by outhousing some of their stock. Shared regional repositories are still being discussed as a possible solution, though it requires little hard thought or elementary economics to see that several regional repositories cannot possibly compare with a single national repository for costs or effectiveness. This particular problem was not anticipated, understood properly, or analysed with a view to identifying the best solution.

If the reaction in the UK was emotional rather than rational, the reaction abroad was no better. Librarians all over the world reacted as if Atkinsonism was some kind of contagious disease that would infect their countries too if some antidote were not found. The report was seen as a threat to their stocks, though the precise nature of the threat in particular countries was rarely specified. Perhaps their bibliothecal manhood felt threatened by the idea of Premature Stock Withdrawal, or Collectio Interrupta. Most of all, perhaps, it was seen as an attack on libraries, though why the UGC should attack libraries was not clear. In fact, if the UGC had not worked out a policy for dealing with a very real problem, it is doubtful whether the British libraries that subsequently received money for new buildings would have done so: it was rarely pointed out that the guidelines laid down were *better* than several libraries had, and allowed them to make a good case for more accommodation. In any case, the Atkinson Report was an attempt to find a solution to the problem in the U.K., not a universal solution.

Another example is very much with us all today. Budgets are not keeping pace with the volume and cost of publications. It would not have been easy to foresee this by more than a few years, but there were warning signs in the mid-1970s and some pretty strong signals by 1980. In view of this, it is hard to sympathize with the panic reactions - not too strong a word - of some librarians faced with a sudden cut. Public libraries, on the principle perhaps of 'last in first out', have often cut out their growing audiovisual services, not on the grounds of present and likely future demand but because they are an easy coherent chunk of activity to chop. Academic libraries first of all reduced their book acquisitions because they could not bear the thought of breaking journal runs, even though books probably have a greater browsing value than journals (so that local open access is more important) and are much less easy and convenient to obtain on interlibrary loan. When they discovered that if they went on doing this they would soon be buying no books at all - some nearly reached this situation - they started cutting journals - some by asking academic staff what they thought, some by sacrificing titles likely to cause least trouble, some on the basis of actual use studies, usually carried out over too short a period to yield really valid data. Is it too much to expect that they might have started to collect good data on use at least a year or two in advance of having to make cancellations, and related these to costs, not only purchase price but processing, binding and storage costs, so that journals were ranked in order of cost per use? There would of course be other factors to be taken into account, but the basic hard facts ought to be available. Incidentally, how many organizations could survive a continued inability to supply no more than 60 or 70 percent of items wanted by customers within 24 hours?

On a broader front, cuts lead libraries to talk about 'resource sharing' - *talk* about it rather that *do* anything about it, because on examination (or even after prolonged discussion) it soon becomes clear that it is exceedingly hard to find any kind of 'resource sharing' that yields half as much as it costs, in staff time, effort and hard cash. There are other alternatives to national provision than the sharing of resources among libraries, but these are rarely looked at because librarians have not even identified the problem as one of national provision; rather, they seem to have picked up a current catch phrase, or perhaps reacted with a sort of knee-jerk reflex - conditioned by 'conventional wisdom', so often a synonym for intellectual laziness. In fact, librarians make the worst of all worlds, because not only do they do little about resource sharing (and what they do is mostly costly and ineffective) but they have wasted time and money discussing the wrong problem. (It is noteworthy that one of the first reactions of librarians to shortage of money is to spend money on discussing with other librarians how to deal with the shortage of money, but there are few things librarians enjoy more than frequent, extensive and inconclusive discussions).

As for national document provision and supply, I have visited quite a few countries, looking at their interlending systems more or less closely - in some cases very closely - and am amazed at the regularity with which they arrive at conclusions ('solutions' would be the wrong word) that are at best sub-optimal and at worst pessimal, as if their aim was to maximize the ratio of costs to effectiveness. In some countries an economic and effective solution to a very real problem is clearly visible, but is scrupulously avoided. Australia affords a particularly fine example of this. Its document supply problem is generally recognized; it has been the subject of several papers and two conferences in the last seven years alone. In Canberra stands the National Library, with a very large collection of current journals, grossly underused because Canberra is not a main centre of population or research and has no industry. Problem and solution are perfectly matched, but they do not meet.

Why does this sort of thing happen? Sometimes a committee of librarians, most of them with their own special interests or axes to grind, is set up, or a research study is commissioned and then put before the library community to discuss. In either case the result is much the same: a compromise that does not upset too many people and that does not solve the problem either. More often no serious attempt is made to tackle the problem, librarians perhaps believing, cynically but realistically, that it is better to spend no time and effort reaching no solution than to set up committees and research studies to reach a non-solution.

Resource Sharing is one trendy concept. Bibligraphic Networking is another. This is founded on two totally unproven assumptions: that there is a standard and extensive catalogue record that is appropriate for all libraries, and that it is more cost-effective to obtain catalogue records from a cooperative or national file than to make them in one's own library. AACR2 is one of the most remarkable examples of trying to solve a problem by committee, with predictable results. The committee did not even tackle the right problem - what *users* surely want is not comprehensive or perfectly accurate bibliographic records, but far better subject access to books, comparable with that provided for scientific journal articles by the large international databases. No data on users' needs, whether for bibliographic information or subject access, were collected; instead, *cataloguers* discussed how to change the rules, rather as if hens were to gather together to discuss the design of eggs. I am however doing the committee an injustice in accusing them of not involving consumers in their discussions, because much of the use made of catalogues is in fact by cataloguers for the purpose of adding to them. Cataloguers would lose their status if it were shown that most cataloguing is a trivial job easily done by clerical staff or that the length of a catalogue entry was not a sign of virility. The research reported several years ago into long vs short records by the Centre for Catalogue Research at Bath University poses two serious questions about both AACR2 and MARC records. Why was not such research carried out years ago? Why is discussion by groups of librarians, however distinguished, preferred to the collection of relevant facts?

Our attempts to deal with subject access to books have been particularly ill-directed. We have heralded as major advances additional complexities in already complex classification schemes or sophisticated subject indexing methods like PRECIS that may represent conceptual breakthroughs but that are in practice virtually useless because no-one can afford to use them. Why not

43

experiment, for example, with keyword searching on content pages fed into the computer? Such a system would contain a lot of 'noise' and miss quite a lot, but it would give us, very cheaply, far better subject access than we have now. Why must we always go for the unattainable 100 per cent, and spend vast resources we don't have getting nowhere near it, when we could reach 70 per cent with quite modest resources?

I would like to see a totally different approach to catalogue records of books, based on what is needed for local housekeeping and access, what files (and what sort of files) are desirable for locating materials elsewhere, what is needed for bibliographic searching (e.g. to check references) and what is needed for decent subject access. National databases as at present conceived seem likely to fulfil none of these desiderata very well. The third and fourth needs could probably be best satisfied by international databases, the first by simple local records, and the second by a specially designed national file, whose nature would be largely determined by the national document supply system.

I am not saying that my alternative approach to catalogue records is right, or that it is the only sensible alternative. What I am saying is that I have seen little or no sign in the literature or elsewhere of a thorough analysis of the needs and issues involved or of any attempt to conceive of alternative approaches. Instead we have the good old tradition of assumed needs and largely preconceived solutions. Again there is a failure to identify the problem, a failure to imagine possible solutions, a failure to collect the information needed to help find the best solution, and a failure to analyse fully what data and proposed solutions are available. If the best solution were by any accident found, I have little doubt that the initiative and courage necessary to implement it would be lacking.

Yet another current buzzword is Conservation. Numerous librarians all over the world have been bitten by the conservation bug. I am all in favour of conservation so long as it does not become an obsession and push other essential functions of libraries into subsidiary positions. However, it is usually assumed that what should first be conserved is the ordinary bound book - older before more recent, non-fiction before fiction. But if I were a historian I would have little interest in an edition of Macaulay's History of England or many other standard books of the nineteenth (or any other) century; I would be much more interested in the ephemera of the day, broad-sheets, pamphlets and local newspapers - material that is usually the last to be collected, let alone conserved. Have historians actually been consulted? And if not, why not?

I could offer many other examples to illustrate my thesis. If almost any major (or for that matter minor) issue in librarianship is examined in any depth, one is forced to question the conventional approach; the standard answers will rarely stand up to close scrutiny. It is particularly sad to see developing countries, with their very limited resources, straining to follow models in developed countries that are inappropriate even in developed countries and irrelevant to themselves.

I would add that I am conscious of a serious general lack of incisive thinking, an inability to cut through the flannel and penetrate to the essential issues, an incapacity to see and tackle issues as *management* problems. For example, libraries have so much in the way of resources, of staff, money, stock and buildings. The questions are first, what is the best one can do with these resources, and second, how solid a case can be made for more resources if, even when optimized, they are genuinely not enough to serve users. It is criminal to stand by rigid cataloguing codes (even if they were soundly based) if this means the existence and even growth of a backlog of books awaiting processing. If such a stand is made for long enough, it may well prove to be Cutter's Last Stand.

I realized when I came to prepare my notes for this paper that the title I had chosen was incomplete, for not only have librarians failed to use their intellect and imagination, but they have failed to put their users before themselves and their stocks. How else can one explain catalogues designed for cataloguers, classification schemes designed for who knows what or whom (certainly not users), library systems that are so difficult to use that instead of making them simpler librarians have the impertinence of 'educating' people to use them? How else explain the huge backlogs of current books that remain inaccessible in many libraries because librarians will not depart in the slightest degree from perfectionist cataloguing standards? How else explain bibliographers playing with their bibliographic tools while users remain unsatisfied? How else explain the common practice of sending journals to the binder for several weeks at the time of maximum demand? How else explain the mystification, the pseudo-professionalism, the status-seeking of librarians? How else explain our so-called professional education, which inculcates knowledge that is either irrelevant or likely to be out of date in 3 or 4 years, while failing to recruit or develop the qualities of imagination and analytical ability and the spirit of *service* that we need so badly? Librarianship as it is practised is a failure of *humanity* as well as of intellect and imagination.

Why, for that matter, should we be talking about *librarianship* at all? If one thing is clear to me, it is that the boundaries, never as clear cut as was supposed, are becoming rapidly eroded. On the other side of our self-constructed (and defensive?) walls are several other major activities: publishing, bookselling, broadcasting, telecommunications, computer processing, even advertising. Unless we can see our future in a far broader context we may not have a future. We need a wide-angle as well as a telescopic lens. Our territory is being lost while we think we are defending it, because we are defending the form and not the substance, and the substance is changing.

In order to see our future in a broader context, we have to go back to fundamentals: to look at the nature and needs of our future society - always bearing in mind that society consists of individual human beings; to look at likely future information needs - not merely research information but leisure needs; to explore how these could be met, bearing in mind the great advances in storing, retrieving and transmitting information of all kinds; and finally to see whether and how anything that we would recognize as librarianship fits into the picture. In public librarianship in particular a radical rethink seems to me to be quite urgently needed, since this is closest to the body of society; but all kinds of librarians - including national librarians - need to reassess their role. In doing so we shall at various points have to work together with our neighbours in publishing, telecommunications and so on. After all, it should be more interesting and exciting to operate in a larger area than our own small patch, the soil of which soon becomes exhausted without constant doses of fertilizer.

I have said little directly about the failure of initiative, though it is implicit in much of the above. One indication of this failure is our habit of waiting till problems are upon us before we react, and then blaming someone else. More profoundly, the way librarians have missed opportunities and seen their province gradually diminish is symptomatic - the early reactions of academic librarians to computerized database searching are one example of this. One of the biggest tests of initiative is about to come. Up to now librarians have competed largely with one another, and this has been easy enough - so easy that we are ill-prepared to face the competition from the private sector that will undoubtedly become more and more prominent as information comes to be regarded more and more as a commercial commodity to be subjected to the laws of a market economy. This is far too big an issue to discuss here, but it will demand all the initiative and leadership we can muster. If we are to judge by the leadership we have mustered in the past, we shall not do very well.

I return to my first statement: libraries are being cut back at the same time as our countries are moving towards an information society. Obviously we have not made a persuasive case to government* - although, in spite of all our deficiencies, we do have

----

* An excellent example of our failure is provided by the report of the Government's Information Technology Advisory Panel, Making a business of information (HMSO, 1983). This ostensibly set out to redress a former bias towards technology by focussing on information, but, barely mentioned libraries. Again, the term 'added value' is common currency in the information world; but precious little attention is paid to the resources to which value would be added.

a powerful case to make. Let us use our energies in making it, rather than in defending what we happen to be doing now, trying to hold on to unused publications that libraries no longer have room to house, having theological arguments about the contents of catalogue records, and indulging in the numerous other irrelevant, inappropriate or trivial activities of which librarians are so fond, with their unerring eye for the inessential. If you think I am exaggerating, look at the large amount of library literature published in the UK, the USA, or in any other country in the last four or five years, and see how many writings you can find that deal with the major issues that will affect our future. You will not find more than a few. In even fewer will you find any sense of *excitement* at being part of a set of key activities that are crucial to the future of our societies. While the future of libraries is in the melting pot, librarians seem to be in a state of moral, social and political confusion. All over the world we have the unappealing picture of librarians contemplating their navels and holding on to their fallacies.

Some of the issues I have raised are national and should be tackled at a national level; some are local. It would however be a cop-out for local librarians to leave national issues to others. It is too easy to say 'these matters are too big for little me; somebody else should do something about them' (the SESDSAT syndrome); nobody may do anything about them unless there is pressure at the grass roots (the force exerted by growing grass is remarkably strong), and if somebody up there does try and do something it is unlikely to work unless a lot of people down here are willing and able to put a programme into action. (Every boss, however powerful, knows that his staff are able to obstruct or dilute almost anything he tries to get done and may well do so unless he gains their understanding and support). Nor is the solution to national problems a sort of Superbody, as some have advocated - 'what we need is a body with teeth'. This Superbody would, its advocates hope, be programmed and operated by them, and its teeth would be permanently facing, if not gnashing at, others, people about whom something should be done. The fact is of course that if it had real teeth they would be sharp Government teeth, not NHS false teeth that could be taken out if they caused trouble. We need national advocates for librarianship; we do not need national guards.

It may be objected that my strictures on librarianship could be applied to almost any job or activity. To this I would reply not only that weakness in other areas is a very feeble excuse for weakness in one's own, but that our situation is more serious. Few people regard librarianship as an essential job such as teaching, nursing, or for that matter plumbing. Anyway, why have museums made such enormous progress in the last three decades, to a point where many are now so popular that they can operate as commercial concerns? At the same time as new challenges and opportunities are appearing, we are seeing territory that we should be interested in holding, if not extending, being eroded or taken over by others. In the long term this may not matter so long as society is served adequately with information; but if the private sector takes over it may not be. In any case I doubt if many librarians actually want to annihilate their jobs, though some of them seem to be doing their best to accelerate the process. ('It's downhill all the way from here,' as the Gadarene swine said).

If we are to make a case, energy and leadership will not be enough: to prepare it we shall need all the intellect and imagination upon which we can call; and all we do must ultimately be in the service of human beings. I may have sounded pessimistic, but I simply do not believe that librarianship does not have somewhere among its practitioners enough of the qualities of intellect, imagination, initiative - and humanity - that are needed if we are to help to shape our future. Somehow we have to find ways of bringing them out, bringing them together, and *using* them. We have nothing to lose but our mental laziness, our spiritual dullness, our introspection and our inhibitions.

With these ringing phrases this paper should end, and did in its primal version. But reactions from individuals to this first version prompted a coda. Not only was there support for my views from librarians at middle and lower management levels, but I was conscious of a large reservoir of energy and enthusiasm waiting to be tapped - and waiting in vain. Is it possible that it is being held back, not deliberately but by default, by senior management? Are there perhaps some chiefs who spend most of their time and energy coping with their committees, sitting on platforms at conferences, participating in national committees of more or (usually) less value, and travelling the globe telling other countries what to do - rather than seeing it as one of their main responsibilities to develop as many of their staff as possible as fully as possible, preferably to a level better than themselves? Is the road to professional advancement seen by many as the pursuit of convention and the avoidance of heresy, so that in due course young turks turn into old mandarins - a kind of reverse miracle of turning wine into water?

There is an alternative and much gloomier possibility, that while younger librarians are quite ready to criticize their seniors, they do not want to assume responsibility themselves; they diagnose but do not wish to cure, content as so many are when confronted by huge problems to live their own lives as quietly as possible - a kind of social despair, manifested most clearly in the cynicism of people towards politics, as if politics were something entirely separate, which did not concern them at all. The world may be hard to improve, but it is easy to make it worse - and cynical inactivity contributes to making it worse. Librarianship is not politics, and information and its communication are not the world, but the same considerations apply. Either we believe in what we are doing or we do not; and if we do we should act on our beliefs.

References

1. University Grants Committee. *Capital provision for university libraries : report of a working party.* London : HMSO, 1976.

2. Seal, Alan & others. *Full and short entry catalogues : library needs and uses.* Bath : University Library, Centre for Catalogue Research, 1982.

This piece (previously unpublished, and first given as a paper in Sydney in 1983; revised in 1987) is included not because it is (or is intended to be) funny but because it has not previously been published - and is possibly unpublishable in any respectable journal.

50

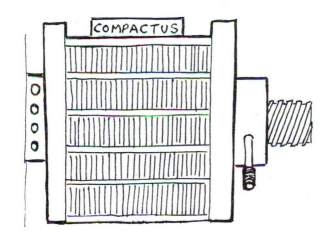

COMPACTUS

ISLiP: AN IMAGINATIVE VENTURE

Eunice M Blair

This is a first report of an interesting and potentially important project in Iceland. It has been kept fairly quiet since its inception 5 years ago, for reasons that may become clear later, but it is thought that a useful service would now be rendered by publication of the results, since they may have valuable lessons to teach others.

Iceland has a population of only 250,000, but a substantial book production. Clearly each book can have only a limited market, since almost no-one outside Iceland can read Icelandic, so the price of books is fairly high and the development of the book industry is inhibited.

However, there are sheep as well as people in Iceland: five sheep to every person, in fact. Seven or eight years ago an imaginative librarian did a piece of lateral thinking: if sheep could be taught to read, there could be a very large increase in the market, which would benefit libraries as well as publishers. He talked to some farmers, whose help was engaged, and so evolved the Icelandic Sheep Literary Project - ISLiP. A project director was appointed and the experiment started in 1980.

Some difficulties were foreseen from the beginning. Sheep are not the most intelligent of animals, and any kind of learning was likely to come hard to them, let alone independent learning. It proved very hard to get them to distinguish reading materials as physical objects from anything but grass - in fact, some prototype ovine literature was eaten by them, with results that were beneficial neither to the sheep nor to the literature. Early attempts to provide even the simplest reading matter on paper proved futile. Apart from anything else, the sheep had very little time for reading, since most of their day was occupied in eating.

Here the project director took another lateral leap. If the sheep would not go to reading matter, reading matter must be brought to the sheep - and not only brought to them, but put under their noses among the grass while they ate. The reading matter obviously had to be hard wearing, suitable for sticking in the ground, inedible, and also short and simple. Two hundred metal notices that met these basic requirements were therefore ordered from England. Unfortunately the precise purpose of the notices was not stated; and although the sheep were not being trained to read English it was thought undesirable to use the KEEP OFF THE GRASS signs that arrived.

Little by little, with immense effort and a great deal of trial and error, some progress was visible. A few sheep proved slightly brighter than the others, and began to pick up a few words. This was discovered by the smug look on their faces, their evident boredom with the existing reading material and the (relative) avidity with which they took to new matter. The leader of the Advanced Reading Group was a strong as well as intelligent ram, called Rambo Ramsson. A younger male, Lari Lambsson, also proved quite keen. The ewes were slower, partly because the production of lambs took up some of their time; the best was Ewe Ewesdottir.

The problem was now what to give them to read next. They were still inclined to eat rather than read anything on paper, and it was expensive providing inedible reading matter. On the other hand, ephemeral media like chalk on blackboards tended to be washed away by the rain, but this was solved by covering the boards with plastic sheeting. As for the contents, these were very short and simple stories about enterprising or productive sheep - productive either of wool or of more sheep; meat was not mentioned for obvious reasons.

However, Rambo and Lari soon grew impatient and showed in various ways that they were dissatisfied. More reading material was produced. At this stage the project director began to get a bit worried, as the sheep were not spending enough time eating and sleeping and developed a lean and hungry look. One day a major breakthrough occurred. Rambo began to copy the letters himself; in a patch of bare ground he scratched clumsily with his foot/hoof 'I love yew'. No one was sure whether he meant the tree (unlikely), or, since his spelling was not yet good, one particular female sheep (even less likely), or ewes in general - but it was certainly progress. After that he spent more and more time scratching on the ground, watched attentively by Lari; the spelling was so erratic, not to mention the syntax, that the project director couldn't understand what was meant, but Lari seemed to. They both got more and more wild-eyed and their wool became more and more scraggy; Rambo even lost his interest in ewes, but there was no question of moving such remarkable sheep from the flock.

Then two surprising things happened. Lari discovered that all the exhortations to reproductivity were of no use or relevance to him, as he had in his early days been deprived of the ability to reproduce. He showed increasing signs of disturbance. Just after he had made this discovery Rambo and he broke into the farmhouse kitchen and went off with some newspapers. The small print and unfamiliar words caused them trouble and it took several weeks of surreptitious reading before they made much sense of it. More scratching on the ground followed, but no sense could be made of it, and it was assumed that Rambo was merely indulging in woolly thinking.

Shortly afterwards Rambo, with Lari at his side, was seen holding what appeared to be meetings with groups of sheep. They would stand in the middle of some grazing sheep and communicate by frantic bleats, echoed by muted bleats from the sheep. It was at this stage that the project director discovered not only that papers had been stolen from the farmhouse but that the *Icelandic Sheep Farmer* was among them. It was very dirty and had obviously been the object of much attention. It included articles on the price of wool and also, more significantly, on the age at which rams should be gelded and the price of lamb and mutton. The project director realized what was happening.

Rambo and Lari disappeared next day and were never seen again. The skills of the other sheep were too poor to hold out much hope of continuing the project, which was abandoned.

The project director, and the instigator of the enterprise, were obviously disappointed, but nevertheless gratified that the project had got so far. The publishing and bookselling trade got nothing out of it, and the farmer expelled the project director from the site. However, he has not given up: he has just gone to India to try to educate cows. Since these cannot be slaughtered, he believes that there is little to stand in the way of success.

Reprinted from:

[Eunice M. Blair] ISLiP: an imaginative venture. *New Library World,* 87 (1038), October 1986, 186-187.

THE JOY OF BACKLOGS

Eunice M Blair

In all the voluminous literature on librarianship, one topic has been almost entirely ignored, although it is a major feature in most libraries and the most conspicuous one in many. This topic is *library backlogs,* which have been so much accepted as a fact of life that no-one bothers to write about them. It is therefore reassuring to learn that serious interest is being shown at last.

Invitations recently went out to the First International Conference on Library Backlogs, which took place in September 1985. At least, it would have done, but unfortunately invitations went out two years late as a result of backlogs of work among the organizers. However, that the topic is of worldwide interest is shown by the acceptances that have already come in; more are expected when those invited have cleared sufficient of their backlogs to read the invitation.

The conference programme as planned makes interesting reading. The first session was devoted to the Uses of Backlogs. As the speakers would have explained, so far from being an accident of nature, an accumulation that creeps up on librarians unawares like a malignant growth, backlogs serve several valuable purposes and should therefore be retained or extended, in some circumstances at least. Advances include the permanent ability to plead understaffing and lack of processing space; job security, in that there is always work waiting to be done, and job satisfaction, in that selection can be made from the backlog of work to suit the tastes of staff; and, perhaps greatest of all, the frustration of readers who have little or no access to recent acquisitions or to staff to whom they wish to turn for help, and the sense of power that this gives librarians.

The second session was entitled An Anatomy of Backlogs. In this, the various types of backlog and their various features would have been described in detail. The best known and most conspicuous type of backlog is the cataloguing backlog, which can lead to vast quantities of books awaiting processing. Since these take up room and almost certainly overflow into other areas, they can also serve as excuses for backlogs of work in other areas. Almost equally satisfying is the acquisition backlog - books awaiting ordering. This should not grow so large that the cataloguing backlog begins to fall to dangerously low levels; nor should delays be so great that books go out of print, for it obviously depletes the cataloguing backlog when books do not arrive. A careful balance needs to be maintained to ensure optimal levels of both acquisition and cataloguing backlogs. Binding backlogs can also be fruitful of chaos and user frustration. There are of course many other kinds of backlogs, from the chief's correspondence through inter-library loan requests to routine desk enquiries.

The third session was concerned with an International Overview. One speaker would have proposed an International Inventory of Cataloguing Backlogs, kept on the computer and updated every year to keep pace with whatever movement occurred. Another (European) speaker would have advocated a European Communities approach - the building, with the aid of CEC funding, of a European Cataloguing Backlog Mountain, parallel to the Butter Mountain and the Wine Lake (with either of which it could perhaps be merged). Finally in this session, an International Exchange of Cataloguing Backlogs would have been suggested. This could take place at random since the books would remain inaccessible wherever they were.

These three rather general sessions were followed in the programme by more technical ones. One of these was entitled The Measurement of Backlogs; it was mainly concerned with cataloguing backlogs. One measure suggested was linear metres of shelving occupied, but the second speaker would have opposed this because many backlogs are not shelved; he would have advocated metric tonnes or cubic metres.

Performance Measurement followed. The most obvious measure is net growth, but ideally more sophsticated techniques are needed to measure movement. 'Backlog flow analysis' was the title of one paper, which suggested similar methods to those used for the flow of slow moving glaciers. One particularly interesting measure is the ratio of backlog to processed stock, since this would enable libraries of different sizes to be compared; another possible ratio is backlog:intake.

In the Backlog Management and Development session speakers would have considered ways of maintaining and increasing backlogs, for example by using elaborate processing methods such as putting stamps on pages 11, 22, 33, 44, 55..., complex cataloguing rules, and very detailed classification with many analyticals. It might seem at first sight that few libraries have much to learn, but at the least some useful tips would have been passed on. As one speaker would have said, the holding of the conference itself would have contributed to the growth of backlogs (is this the real motive behind the enormous growth of conferences, seminars and workshops in recent years?). The organization of backlogs so as to make them almost unmanageable has also reached a high level of sophistication - for example, in a good cataloguing backlog books will be untraceable, in a good correspondence backlog individual letters will be buried, and so on; but here too there is bound to be something more to be learnt.

Backlog Erosion might have been expected to attract less interest, but one of the papers on the programme was unusual. This was by a geneticist who had specialized in breeding large and voracious bookworms and termites (as appropriate to the climate). He believed he had cultivated some new species which could eat through large backlogs in a matter of months. The problem with this solution, as another speaker would have pointed out, is that it is not easy to ensure that the creatures restrict themselves to backlogs. Indeed, in an experiment in one library they ate all the processed stock and half the catalogue over one weekend. In another, they started eating some of the more sedentary staff before they were noticed. However, as yet another speaker would have said, all these supposed problems would have had the effect of increasing backlogs all over the library; a huge cataloguing backlog could be created by ordering vast numbers of replacement books and replacing the last catalogue entries, and staff lost would also have led to greatly increased backlogs. It seems that the geneticist's new breeds would be welcomed only if they were either indiscriminate or could preferably be directed to other things in the library than the backlogs.

In contrast, the session on Enemies of Backlogs would probably have attracted general agreement. The obvious enemies are commonsense, efficiency, and concern with users; and ways of overcoming these handicaps would have been discussed, including the suggestion that staff who continued after warnings to exhibit any of the above hostile characteristics should be asked to leave (preferably the profession, and not just the library where they were doing damage). The governments of many countries are both enemies of backlogs in that they are cutting acquisition funds and friends in that they are also cutting staff; with good management, libraries should be able to do more to increase backlogs by having fewer staff than to erode them by a smaller intake.

Finally, a rather lighter note would have been struck. The last session was devoted to Backlog Promotion and Publicity. Examples of some striking posters were given in the programme, incorporating such slogans as BACKLOGS ARE THE BACKBONE OF BIBLIOGRAPHY and BACKLOGS ARE BEAUTIFUL. T-shirts had been designed with I'M BACKING BACKLOGS and MY BACKLOG IS BIGGER THAN YOURS on them. A well-known secondhand dealer, parading under the pseudonym of Bach and Logg, offered a prize for the Biggest Cataloguing Backlog as measured in cubic metres. The prize was to add to it the Second Biggest Cataloguing Backlog, for the transport of which the dealer would have paid. An annual competition to choose Miss Backlog would have been initiated, the winner to be the lady with the most impressive backlog figure.

Details were not forgotten in the organization. For example, breakfast would have been eaten at lunch, lunch at dinner, and dinner at breakfast, because of backlogs in cooking and washing up. Beds would have been made in the evening, in some cases after the members of the conference had gone to bed. A novel dance was initially planned where the band would have been two numbers behind the dancers, but this was not considered practicable.

All in all, serious discussion of Backlogs seems now to have a real future. We can expect new titles to appear in the literature such as *First steps in backlogging* and *Fifty years among the backlogs of central Europe.* CONSPECTUS has an obvious application to backlogs both nationally and internationally.

I must get back to my own backlog, which has been growing while I have been writing this.

Reprinted from:

[Eunice M. Blair] The joy of backlogs. *New Library World,* January 1988.

INDEX

by Joyce Line

E

F

G

I

L

M

N